Farm Animals

Los animales de la granja

FIRST EDITION
Series Editor Deborah Lock; **Designer** Sadie Thomas; **US Editor** Elizabeth Hester;
Pre-Production Producer Nadine King; **Producer** Sara Hu;
DTP Designer Almudena Díaz and Pilar Morales; **Jacket Designer** Simon Oon;
Reading Consultant Linda Gambrell, PhD

THIS EDITION
Editorial Management by Oriel Square
Produced for DK by WonderLab Group LLC
Jennifer Emmett, Erica Green, Kate Hale, *Founders*

Editors Grace Hill Smith, Libby Romero, Michaela Weglinski; **Spanish Translation** Isabel C. Mendoza;
Photography Editors Kelley Miller, Annette Kiesow, Nicole DiMella;
Managing Editor Rachel Houghton; **Designers** Project Design Company;
Researcher Michelle Harris; **Copy Editor** Lori Merritt; **Indexer** Connie Binder;
Proofreaders Carmen Orozco, Larry Shea; **Reading Specialist** Dr. Jennifer Albro;
Curriculum Specialist Elaine Larson

Published in the United States by DK Publishing
1745 Broadway, 20th Floor, New York, NY 10019
Copyright © 2023 Dorling Kindersley Limited
DK, a Division of Penguin Random House LLC
23 24 25 26 27 10 9 8 7 6 5 4 3 2 1
001–336106–Aug/2023

A catalog record for this book
is available from the Library of Congress.
HC ISBN: 978-0-7440-8375-0
PB ISBN: 978-0-7440-8374-3

DK books are available at special discounts when purchased
in bulk for sales promotions, premiums, fundraising, or
educational use. For details, contact: DK Publishing Special Markets,
1745 Broadway, 20th Floor, New York, NY 10019
SpecialSales@dk.com

Printed and bound in China

The publisher would like to thank the following for their kind permission to reproduce their images:
a=above; c=center; b=below; l=left; r=right; t=top; b/g=background

123RF.com: Olga Itina 24-25; **Agefotostock.com:** imagebroker 14-15; **Dreamstime.com:** Melanie Hobson 12cl;
Shutterstock.com: Bigandt.com 15t

Cover images: *Front:* **Dreamstime.com:** Kateryna Firsova b; **Shutterstock.com:** Merggy, Pogorelova Olga crb;
Back: **Dreamstime.com:** Ernest Akayeu cla

All other images © Dorling Kindersley

For the curious
Para los curiosos
www.dk.com

Farm
Animals

Los animales de la
granja

Come and meet my friends on the farm.

Ven a conocer a mis amigos de la granja.

farmhouse
casa del granjero

barn
granero

feathers
plumas

chickens

pollos

Here is the chicken
with her little chicks.

Aquí está la gallina
con sus pollitos.

chick
pollito

Here is the turkey coming to meet you.

Aquí viene el pavo a saludarte.

snood
zarzo

 **turkeys**

pavos

feathers
plumas

Here is the pig.
Here are three pink piglets.

Aquí está el cerdo.
Aquí hay tres cerditos
rosados.

piglet
cerdito

pigs
cerdos

ear
oreja

11

Here are the cows looking at you.

Aquí están las vacas, mirándote.

udder
ubre

 **cows**

vacas

calf
ternero

hoof
pezuña

Here is the dog. Here are her sleepy puppies.

Aquí está la perra. Aquí están sus cachorros adormilados.

nose
hocico

puppy
cachorro

dogs

perros

Here is the sheep
with two little lambs.

Aquí está la oveja con
dos corderitos.

lamb
cordero

sheep

ovejas

wool
lana

ear
oreja

nose
hocico

goats
cabras

Here is the goat lying down with her kid.

Aquí está la cabra, echada con su cabrito.

kid
cabrito

Here are the ducks with their fluffy ducklings.

Aquí están los patos con sus mullidos patitos.

beak
pico

 **ducks** **patos**

duckling
patito

Here are the white geese looking around.

Aquí están los blancos gansos, mirándolo todo.

geese

gansos

eye
ojo

neck
cuello

Here is the horse running with her foal.

Aquí está la yegua, corriendo con su potro.

horses
caballos

mane
crin

foal
potro

Here are two little ponies.

Aquí hay dos pequeños ponis.

pony
poni

ponies

ponis

Here is the cat curled up with her kitten.

Aquí está la gata, hecha un ovillo con su gatito.

cats

gatos

kitten
gatito

ear
oreja

Come see us
again soon!

¡Regresa pronto
a visitarnos!

Glossary
Glosario

chicken
a bird that is raised by people for its eggs

cow
a large, hoofed animal that is kept for its milk

dog
a four-legged animal that can herd sheep and cows

horse
a hoofed animal used for riding and farm work

sheep
an animal with a thick coat that is raised for wool

caballo
animal con pezuñas que se usa para montar y para trabajar en la granja

oveja
animal de pelo grueso que se cría para obtener lana

perro
animal de cuatro patas que puede pastorear ovejas y vacas

pollo
ave que se cría para obtener huevos

vaca
animal grande con pezuñas que se cría para obtener leche

Quiz
Prueba

Answer the questions to see what you have learned.
Check your answers with an adult.

Which animal am I?

1. I am a baby chicken.
2. I am a pink animal with
    a round snout and big ears.
3. I am a baby cow.
4. I am a baby sheep.
5. I am a bird that likes to swim.

1. A chick 2. A pig (or piglet) 3. A calf 4. A lamb 5. A duck

**Responde las preguntas para saber cuánto aprendiste.
Verifica tus respuestas con un adulto.**

¿Qué animal soy?

1. Soy un pollo bebé.
2. Soy un animal rosado con un hocico redondo
    y orejas grandes.
3. Soy una vaca bebé.
4. Soy una oveja bebé.
5. Soy un ave a la que le gusta nadar.

1. Un pollito 2. Un cerdo (o cerdito) 3. Un ternero 4. Un cordero 5. Un pato